CULTURED

A self-explorative guided journal
for African American males

LOVE

To God, my mom, and my village

Thank you for always believing in me, supporting me, and nurturing my gifts.

To the male that encounters this content, I pray that you ingest, digest, and replicate your greatness to those around you by understanding how valuable you are.

To the mothers that are raising males, I pray that this content will be a guide to help you bond, understand, and embrace his humanity as he continuously develops.

Ingredients

The purpose of this guided journal

This explorative tool will empower African American males to identify and build a healthy relationship with their emotions, which amplifies a human's ability to truly live out their dreams through reflection and reframing.

For decades, African American males have been taught to conform and conditioned to mask their true emotions.

I want to help you explore the inner you as you adopt tools and shed weight that will help to impact the world around you.

The ultimate measure of a man is not where he stands in moments of comfort and convenience, but where he stands at times of challenge and controversy.

- Dr. Martin Luther King, Jr.

Identity and Self-awareness

I am Nasiir Jabari. I was gifted the name that means a strong and powerful helper. A proud servant of God who is called to bring individuals closer to freedom through His love. I am a bold leader who has been entrusted to share wisdom with my generation. A skilled student athlete with an abundance of passion for sports.

I am learning that fitness is my sweet spot. I take pride in becoming a whole person, mentally emotionally, physically, and spiritually. I have been coached since age five to identify and manage tough emotions. In addition, I have been taught breathing techniques and the skill of journaling my way through life.

Safe Space

Bro, take this time to check in with yourself.
Write any thoughts that have crossed your mind so far.

Prompt #1

Your turn, who are you? And what is your purpose in the world?

Reflection and Reframing

Allow these lines to hold your words as you process

Reflection and Reframing

Allow these lines to hold your words as you process

_____

_____

_____

_____

_____

_____

_____

_____

_____

_____

_____

_____

_____

_____

Reflection and Reframing

Allow these lines to hold your words as you process

Safe Space

Bro, take this time to check in with yourself.
Write any thoughts that have crossed your mind so far.

JOY

JOY

The emotion that allows us to be content in favorable and unfavorable circumstances. You can have joy anywhere at any time in the world. I like to think of joy as a best friend or brother because you have an unlimited supply of its presence. You can experience joy when you are crying, driving, walking, or laughing.

I had to learn that even when there is a storm in life, I can still <u>choose </u>to access joy or wait until the storm is over.

Safe Space

Bro, take this time to check in with yourself.
Write any thoughts that have crossed your mind so far.

Prompt #2.

What gives you joy?

Identify the things that you like to do, places
you like to go, and people that you love.

Reflection and Reframing

Allow these lines to hold your words as you process

Reflection and Reframing

Allow these lines to hold your words as you process

_____

_____

_____

_____

_____

_____

_____

_____

_____

_____

_____

_____

_____

_____

_____

_____

_____

Reflection and Reframing

Allow these lines to hold your words as you process

Prompt #3

When was the last time that you experienced joy?

Think about your daily life and the moments when joy is accessed.

Reflection and Reframing

Allow these lines to hold your words as you process

Reflection and Reframing

Allow these lines to hold your words as you process

_____

_____

_____

_____

_____

_____

_____

_____

_____

_____

_____

_____

_____

_____

_____

_____

Reflection and Reframing

Allow these lines to hold your words as you process

Prompt #4

Do you wait for happy or successful moments to experience joy?

Think about your daily life and the moments when you experience or express joy the most.

Reflection and Reframing

Allow these lines to hold your words as you process

_____

_____

_____

_____

_____

_____

_____

_____

_____

_____

_____

_____

_____

_____

_____

_____

_____

_____

_____

_____

Reflection and Reframing

Allow these lines to hold your words as you process

_____

_____

_____

_____

_____

_____

_____

_____

_____

_____

_____

_____

_____

_____

_____

_____

Reflection and Reframing

Allow these lines to hold your words as you process

Prompt #5

Do you give yourself "permission" to experience the joy that is inside of you?

Think about your daily life and if you access joy
in favorable and unfavorable circumstances.

Reflection and Reframing

Allow these lines to hold your words as you process

Reflection and Reframing

Allow these lines to hold your words as you process

_____

_____

_____

_____

_____

_____

_____

_____

_____

_____

_____

_____

_____

_____

_____

_____

Reflection and Reframing

Allow these lines to hold your words as you process

Prompt #6

How easily do you allow people take away your joy?

Think about a time that you may have had an unpleasant experience, your reaction, and recovery.

Reflection and Reframing

Allow these lines to hold your words as you process

Reflection and Reframing

Allow these lines to hold your words as you process

_____

_____

_____

_____

_____

_____

_____

_____

_____

_____

_____

_____

_____

_____

_____

_____

Reflection and Reframing

Allow these lines to hold your words as you process

Safe Space

Bro, take this time to check in with yourself.
Write any thoughts that have crossed your mind so far.

CONFIDENCE

CONFIDENCE

Confidence is a necessary life skill. I learned confidence by embracing my style and uniqueness with different fashion ideas. A lot of boys, young men, and men struggle with confidence simply because of a hiccup in identity. When you and your creator affirm your existence, there is no way your confidence stays limited.

I challenge you to affirm yourself daily. My mother suggested that I listen to an audiobook for Black boys that pours into me daily. The words changed my perspective and the way I show up in the world.

Belief comes from hearing truth. Romans 10:17

Safe Space

Bro, take this time to check in with yourself.
Write any thoughts that have crossed your mind so far.

Prompt #8

What does confidence mean to you?

Think big picture.

Reflect on what the world has taught you
and brainstorm <u>your</u> perception.

Reflection and Reframing

Allow these lines to hold your words as you process

_____

_____

_____

_____

_____

_____

_____

_____

_____

_____

_____

_____

_____

_____

_____

_____

_____

_____

Reflection and Reframing

Allow these lines to hold your words as you process

_____

_____

_____

_____

_____

_____

_____

_____

_____

_____

_____

_____

_____

_____

_____

_____

Reflection and Reframing

Allow these lines to hold your words as you process

Prompt #9

Does your support circle help you with building confidence?

Brainstorm the people and ways that they help you.

Reflection and Reframing

Allow these lines to hold your words as you process

_____

_____

_____

_____

_____

_____

_____

_____

_____

_____

_____

_____

_____

_____

_____

_____

_____

_____

_____

_____

Reflection and Reframing

Allow these lines to hold your words as you process

_____

_____

_____

_____

_____

_____

_____

_____

_____

_____

_____

_____

_____

_____

_____

Reflection and Reframing

Allow these lines to hold your words as you process

Prompt #10

Is confidence a struggle for you?
If so, where is the struggle?

If not, how have you learned to be
strengthened in your confidence?

Reflection and Reframing

Allow these lines to hold your words as you process

_____

_____

_____

_____

_____

_____

_____

_____

_____

_____

_____

_____

_____

_____

_____

_____

_____

Reflection and Reframing

Allow these lines to hold your words as you process

_____

_____

_____

_____

_____

_____

_____

_____

_____

_____

_____

_____

_____

_____

_____

_____

_____

Reflection and Reframing

Allow these lines to hold your words as you process

Prompt #11

How does your confidence affect you in today's society?

Think about the amount of influence that culture, social media, family, and friend's opinions have on your view of self.

Reflection and Reframing

Allow these lines to hold your words as you process

Reflection and Reframing

Allow these lines to hold your words as you process

_____

_____

_____

_____

_____

_____

_____

_____

_____

_____

_____

_____

_____

_____

_____

_____

Reflection and Reframing

Allow these lines to hold your words as you process

Prompt #12

How can your confidence help to break generational cycles and create generational abundance?

Think about the ways that your gifts and confidence collide to push your generation forward.

Reflection and Reframing

Allow these lines to hold your words as you process

Reflection and Reframing

Allow these lines to hold your words as you process

_____

_____

_____

_____

_____

_____

_____

_____

_____

_____

_____

_____

_____

_____

_____

_____

_____

_____

Reflection and Reframing

Allow these lines to hold your words as you process

_____

_____

_____

_____

_____

_____

_____

_____

_____

_____

_____

_____

_____

_____

_____

_____

_____

_____

Safe Space

Bro, take this time to check in with yourself.
Write any thoughts that have crossed your mind so far.

ANGER

ANGER

The emotion that can be daunting and overshadow the male's ability to live fully in who he was created to be. Anger is an emotion that tests you, your abilities, and thought processes. When you have anger it does not define who you are but rather how you feel.

I will transparently share that a few years ago, I was struggling with identity, grew angry and I damaged a wall in my room. It was not until I took time to reset that I realized my emotions felt stuck. In my humanness with accessible tools, I still exploded. My mom did not judge me, she coached me through it by helping me to identify and express this new and big emotion.

Now, I set goals around my emotions to build a healthy relationship, so that I can grow to master the emotions instead of them mastering me.

You anger is not stronger than you

Safe Space

Bro, take this time to check in with yourself.
Write any thoughts that have crossed your mind so far.

Prompt #14

How do you address and process through your anger?

Think about people, places, and
things that help you to cope.

Reflection and Reframing

Allow these lines to hold your words as you process

Reflection and Reframing

Allow these lines to hold your words as you process

Reflection and Reframing

Allow these lines to hold your words as you process

Prompt #15

Do you judge yourself
when you are angry?

Create healthy self-talk to make the moments easier.

Reflection and Reframing

Allow these lines to hold your words as you process

Reflection and Reframing

Allow these lines to hold your words as you process

_____

_____

_____

_____

_____

_____

_____

_____

_____

_____

_____

_____

_____

_____

_____

_____

Reflection and Reframing

Allow these lines to hold your words as you process

_____

_____

_____

_____

_____

_____

_____

_____

_____

_____

_____

_____

_____

_____

_____

_____

Prompt #16

Has anger made you do or say something that you later regretted?

This is your opportunity to shift reactions and responses.

List some new ways of expression.

Reflection and Reframing

Allow these lines to hold your words as you process

_____

_____

_____

_____

_____

_____

_____

_____

_____

_____

_____

_____

_____

_____

_____

_____

_____

Reflection and Reframing

Allow these lines to hold your words as you process

_____

_____

_____

_____

_____

_____

_____

_____

_____

_____

_____

_____

_____

_____

_____

_____

_____

Reflection and Reframing

Allow these lines to hold your words as you process

Prompt #17

How can you build a relationship with your anger?

Think about how you can express this emotion in a healthy way when it comes to challenge you.

Reflection and Reframing

Allow these lines to hold your words as you process

_____

_____

_____

_____

_____

_____

_____

_____

_____

_____

_____

_____

_____

_____

_____

_____

_____

Reflection and Reframing

Allow these lines to hold your words as you process

_____

_____

_____

_____

_____

_____

_____

_____

_____

_____

_____

_____

_____

_____

_____

_____

Reflection and Reframing

Allow these lines to hold your words as you process

_____

_____

_____

_____

_____

_____

_____

_____

_____

_____

_____

_____

_____

_____

_____

_____

_____

_____

Safe Space

Bro, take this time to check in with yourself.
Write any thoughts that have crossed your mind so far.

Literal Terms

Joy

joy

/joi/

noun

1

a feeling of great pleasure and happiness.

Confidence

con·fi·dence

/ˈkänfəd(ə)ns/

noun

1

the feeling or belief that one can rely on someone or something; firm trust.

Anger

an·ger

/ˈaNGgər/

noun

1

a strong feeling of annoyance, displeasure, or hostility.

COMMUNITY

Bro, we may be wrapping up the pages, but we will continue the journey. This is done by getting in community with likeminded individuals. Share your greatness, advocate for yourself and others, and live to your greatest potential. Promise me that you will not only adopt new ways to manage your emotions, but also recite powerful affirmations daily as the King you are and always will be.

I'm rooting for you in the spirit.

- Nasiir

King Affirmations

I will continue to break generational cycles.

I am a leader.

I cannot be stopped.

I am strong mentally, emotionally, physically, and spiritually.

God loves me.

I have joy.

I am cool on the inside and out.

I will make a change each day.

I will reach my goals.

I am different.

A Planted Seed

The depth of your soul and your ability to lead is far greater than I can ever express or imagine.

Godspeed

Mom

Made in the USA
Columbia, SC
18 June 2024

36868155R00052